How Should America Deal with Undocumented Immigrants?

Other titles in the *Issues Today* series include:

How Should America Deal with Undocumented Immigrants?

James Roland

ReferencePoint
Press®

San Diego, CA

ReferencePoint
Press®

For more information, contact:
ReferencePoint Press, Inc.
PO Box 27779
San Diego, CA 92198
www.ReferencePointPress.com

LIBRARY OF CONGRESS CATALOGING-IN-PUBLICATION DATA

Names: Roland, James, author.
Title: How should America deal with undocumented immigrants? / By James Roland.
Description: San Diego, CA : ReferencePoint Press, Inc., [2021] | Series:
   Issues today | Includes bibliographical references and index.
Identifiers: LCCN 2020017079 (print) | LCCN 2020017080 (ebook) | ISBN
   9781682828816 (library binding) | ISBN 9781682828823 (ebook)
Subjects: LCSH: Illegal aliens--United States--Juvenile literature. |
   Illegal aliens--Government policy--United States--Juvenile literature. |
   United States--Emigration and immigration--Juvenile literature.
Classification: LCC JV6483 .R65 2021 (print) | LCC JV6483 (ebook) | DDC
   325.73--dc23
LC record available at https://lccn.loc.gov/2020017079
LC ebook record available at https://lccn.loc.gov/2020017080

CONTENTS

In and Out of the Shadows

On the morning of August 7, 2019, armed agents with US Immigration and Customs Enforcement (ICE) fanned out across rural Mississippi, entered seven food-processing plants, and arrested about 680 workers suspected of being undocumented immigrants—people living in the country without authorization. It was ICE's largest workplace raid in the state's history.

Many of the plant workers had just kissed their children goodbye before the first day of school. By the afternoon, those same kids were wondering whether they would see their moms and dads again. "I need my dad. . . . He's not a criminal,"[1] a crying little girl told a local television news crew.

About half of the people arrested were released within the first twenty-four hours, but others spent weeks and months in custody, navigating the criminal justice system and immigration courts on their way toward deportation. Among those workers was a woman named Elisa, who was the mother of three young children. She spent forty-nine days in custody before being released, her future status in the United States uncertain. "Whenever I leave the house, my little boy worries if I'll come home," she told National Public Radio through an interpreter, adding that the Latino community in the small town of Morton, Mississippi, is equally frightened. "A lot of people aren't leaving the house. The truth is nothing will be the same here. Now we're just living with fear."[2]

Although ICE officials and others concerned about the presence of undocumented immigrants may understand the anxiety associated with living in the United States without authorization, they say the issue boils down simply to right and wrong. Jere Miles, the ICE special agent in charge of the region that includes Mississippi, says undocumented immigrants living and working in the United States are here illegally and ICE's job is to enforce the nation's immigration laws. "Whether you've been here a week, a month or 10 years, you're still violating the law,"[3] he says.

> "Whenever I leave the house, my little boy worries if I'll come home."[2]
>
> —Elisa, an undocumented immigrant

And therein lies the enormous challenge facing the nation, from small towns in Mississippi to Congress and the White House: how should America deal with undocumented immigrants? There are an estimated 11 million undocumented immigrants in the United States. They make up a varied melting pot of personalities, occupations, and experiences. They go to school. They raise families. They work in restaurants, factories, hospitals, offices, and salons; on farms; and in communities in all fifty states. They are journalists, chefs, nurses, landscapers, painters, mechanics, sales professionals, and much more. America's undocumented immigrants are children, parents, grandparents, and people who often live in

Suspected undocumented immigrants await their fate after ICE raided the Mississippi poultry-processing plant where they worked. ICE raided seven of the state's food-processing plants in August 2019.

fear of having their status revealed and their worlds turned upside down. The worry about being arrested and deported back to their native countries never leaves millions of people who otherwise hope for a better, safer life in the United States.

Yet federal laws are clear that immigrants who are in the United States without proper documentation can be deported. Legal immigration, with its regimented system of work visas, asylum protections, and pathways to citizenship, allows the government to maintain some control over the number of new arrivals. This is important because governments, especially at the local and state levels, need to manage their resources to provide for their residents. For example, school districts need to keep close track of the number of students they have in order to hire enough teachers and maintain enough classrooms. Hospitals and public health agencies must be prepared to meet the health needs of everyone living in their communities, regardless of their legal status.

The United States has grappled with how to deal with immigration and undocumented immigrants for more than a century. After all that time, and with millions of people working and living here under the shadow of an uncertain future, the country still has no plans that work for everybody—the families fleeing violence in their homelands; the schools, health care facilities, and communities dealing with an influx of undocumented immigrants; and US citizens concerned about how their tax dollars are being spent on immigrants and how the influx of immigrants is changing the nation.

Lawmakers, activists, and many others wrestle with the subject year after year. Immigration reform is a key, controversial issue in state and federal elections. To picture possible solutions, it helps to understand the scope of the issue, its history, how the country deals with undocumented immigrants now, and what options should be considered going forward.

CHAPTER ONE

Who Are the Undocumented Immigrants?

An immigrant is a person who moves from one country to another in order to live there permanently. By definition, an undocumented immigrant is a person who arrived in a foreign country and is living there without legal authorization. This can be a person who entered the country without legal permission or someone who had documentation, such as a work visa or a student visa, that has since expired.

Of the estimated 11 million unauthorized immigrants in the United States, about 47 percent are from Mexico. For decades, Mexicans represented the majority of undocumented immigrants. But by 2017, two major changes were under way. More Mexican-born people were returning home than were entering the United States, and the number of people arriving in the United States from the so-called Northern Triangle countries of El Salvador, Guatemala, and Honduras was growing substantially—more than a 25 percent increase between 2007 and 2017.

Nonetheless, the number of migrants from Asian countries is the fastest-growing group of undocumented immigrants in the United States. Since 2010, more Asian immigrants than Latin American immigrants—both documented and undocumented— have entered the United States. And by 2065, the Asian immigrant population is expected to be the largest immigrant population in the nation. The four Asian countries from which the majority of immigrants come to the United States are India, South Korea, the Philippines, and China. While immigrants from Mexico, Central

America, and Asia make up the vast majority of undocumented people in the United States, there are about 2 million unauthorized adults and children in the country from Africa, Europe, South America, and the Caribbean.

Entering the United States

Many undocumented immigrants who currently live in the United States entered the country by unlawfully crossing the US–Mexico border. But since 2010, about two-thirds of undocumented immigrants are people who have entered the country legally and overstayed their visas (not migrants who sneaked across the border), according to the Center for Migration Studies (CMS). This shift raises questions about whether a greater focus of immigration enforcement should be addressing the issue of visa violations rather than hardening the southern border with more fencing and walls. "It is clear from our research that persons who overstay their visas add to the US undocumented population at a higher rate than border crossers. This is not a blip, but a trend which has

Many undocumented immigrants enter the United States legally but then stay longer than their visas allow. They often enter through big-city airports, such as John F. Kennedy International Airport in New York City (pictured).

become the norm," says Donald Kerwin, the executive director of the CMS. "As these numbers indicate, construction of hundreds of more miles of border wall would not address the challenge of irregular migration into our country, far from it."[4]

The CMS reports that about half of undocumented immigrants enter the United States by air with work, tourist, or student visas, only to overstay the dates they are to leave the country as set forth in those visas. But because this group of people arrives legally at airports around the country as individuals or in small numbers, they have attracted little attention from the public or policy makers. They are not massing at the southern border, nor have they been seen scaling walls in California, crossing rivers in Texas, or landing on Florida beaches on makeshift rafts—the images of undocumented immigrants usually depicted in the media. "It's right out there in the news, and you can see people," says Robert Warren, senior fellow with the Center for Migration Studies. "With the overstayers, people will be tourists and they'll come here, and they'll either join relatives or they'll join people they know, and they'll get a job, and they're not visible."[5]

Though they represent a smaller portion of the undocumented immigrant population in the United States, successful border crossers still number in the hundreds of thousands annually. It is difficult to get a reliable estimate of the number of people who illegally enter the country across the southern border. Customs and Border Protection (CBP) reports that about 850,000 unauthorized people were stopped at the border in fiscal year 2019, and an estimated 150,000 adults and children escaped detection while entering the United States. These numbers change significantly from month to month and year to year, based partly on

"It is clear from our research that persons who overstay their visas add to the US undocumented population at a higher rate than border crossers. This is not a blip, but a trend which has become the norm."[4]

—Donald Kerwin, the executive director of the Center for Migration Studies the efforts by Mexican authorities to keep people from crossing into the United States, stepped up efforts by US law enforcement agencies, and a growing number of migrants formally seeking asylum in the United States rather than trying to slip into the country undetected.

Border Crossers

Border crossers are often those fleeing poverty, crime, and violence in their home countries, all in hopes of finding safety, work, and—for many immigrants—a better life for their children. In Honduras, for example, one in five people lives in poverty, and communities throughout the Northern Triangle nations lack enough police officers and government resources to maintain order in areas overrun with violent gangs. Economic desperation and crime are also what has fueled a change in the face of undocumented immigrants. In 2003, family units represented only about 3.6 percent of those apprehended at the border. By 2018, more than 27 percent of the people stopped by CBP were in a family unit.

Rafa Arturo and his family are among those who attempted that crossing or sought asylum at an official port of entry. He was born in El Salvador and crossed illegally as a young man into the United States, where he spent much of his life. After being deported with his family back to El Salvador, he survived being shot by gang members in front of his home. As the father of a five-year-old son named Jacob, Arturo's number-one concern is the safety of his little boy. He wants to get Jacob into the United States, even if it means taking a dangerous journey to the border and crossing illegally again. He explains that school walls in El Salvador are covered with gang messages and kids as young as eight years old are recruited to join. "By all means necessary, as a parent, I'll do whatever it takes to get my son to a next step,"[6] Arturo asserts.

"By all means necessary, as a parent, I'll do whatever it takes to get my son to a next step."[6]

—Rafa Arturo, a Salvadoran father considering fleeing violence by illegally entering the United States

More Families Are Crossing the Border Illegally

According to a 2020 report by the Pew Research Center, apprehensions at the US-Mexico border more than doubled in 2019. A major factor contributing to this large increase is the number of families with children who attempted to cross the border illegally. In 2019, Pew notes, 474,000 family units were apprehended while trying to cross the border. That number represents a dramatic increase from previous years and the largest portion of total apprehensions in 2019.

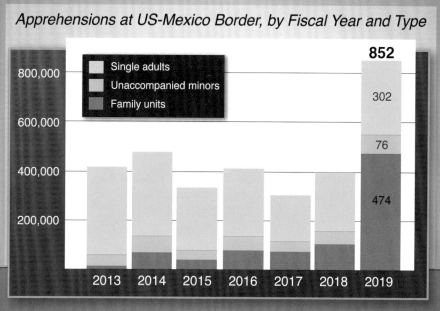

Apprehensions at US-Mexico Border, by Fiscal Year and Type

- Single adults
- Unaccompanied minors
- Family units

Note: "Family units" refers to the number of people traveling in families.

Note: The federal government's fiscal year runs from October 1 through September 30. For example, FY 2019 is between October 1, 2018 and September 30, 2019.

Source: John Gramlich, "How Border Apprehensions, ICE Arrests and Deportations Have Changed Under Trump," Pew Research Center, March 2, 2020. www.pewresearch.org.

Undocumented immigrants who enter the United States by illegally crossing a border normally do so into Texas, New Mexico, Arizona, or California. Some cross on foot in remote areas far from the nearest city, or they pay to be hidden in the back of vans or trucks moving through checkpoints. And although the US–Mexico border is where most undocumented immigrants enter the country, there has been a growing number of illegal crossings on the US-Canada border in recent years. In 2017, US Border

Stopping Smugglers of Human Cargo

The US Coast Guard reports that every year thousands of people try to enter the country by sea. Florida, with its 1,350 miles (2,173 km) of coastline, is an especially popular destination for smugglers who take money from undocumented immigrants to bring them ashore or close to shore. "We are saving lives out there, because a lot of these folks that are running and smuggling human beings into America via maritime means are not doing it in a safe manner," says Lieutenant Commander Kristopher Ensley, the captain of the Coast Guard cutter *Paul Clark*, based in Miami. "They're overloading these boats and trying to sneak people into America."

Many migrants also pay smugglers to get them into the United States by land. In order to avoid law enforcement, smugglers use routes that lead to wilderness areas, where immigrants are left on their own to find food and shelter in the nearest town. In February 2020, three women who had crossed illegally into the United States died after getting lost in the Laguna Mountains of Southern California. "This incident that resulted in the tragic loss of lives was totally avoidable," says Chief Patrol Agent Aaron Heitke with the Border Patrol in San Diego. "We have said many times, do not place your life or the lives of your loved ones in the hands of ruthless smugglers."

Quoted in Samantha-Jo Roth, "Exclusive: Go Inside the Coast Guard's Mission to Intercept Migrants at Sea" Spectrum News 13, November 4, 2019. www.mynews13.com.

Quoted in Alex Riggins, "3 Women Die in Laguna Mountains After Crossing Border Near San Diego," *Los Angeles Times*, February 11, 2020. www.latimes.com.

Patrol agents apprehended 165 people at the northern border, but in 2018 that number rose to 963 migrants, most of them crossing into New Hampshire, Vermont, and New York.

Limited Legal Options

One of the chief reasons why migrants cross the border illegally, knowing they will live a fugitive existence, is that the legal channels to become a documented immigrant are extremely limited. The US government issues about a million permanent resident visas—known as green cards—annually to immigrants for work purposes or family-related reasons. About half of those sought-after visas are given to family members of US citizens or permanent residents. These are granted to spouses and unmarried children of green card holders as well as to immediate family members of US citizens currently living abroad. While nearly half a million family migration visas may sound like a lot, there are more than 13 million green card holders in the United States, many of whom have relatives they want to bring to the country, and there are US citizens who have family members in other countries.

Most work-related green cards go to people in jobs that require a college degree, such as those in technology, medicine, or business. For so-called low-skilled jobs in agriculture or in restaurants, for instance, there are few green cards available. Instead, a limited number of temporary work visas are also available in various fields, such as health care and agriculture. However, they do not come close to meeting the demand from migrants, and they are usually issued for one year at a time, meaning every year a worker faces the uncertainty of getting a temporary visa renewal or having to leave the country.

In addition, green cards and other work visas are unevenly allotted to foreign countries. The US government, through its consulates in each country, issues more visas to those with the greatest demand and fewer to countries that have fewer people seeking to work in the United States. For example, about 160,000 green cards are issued to people from Mexico each year, but only 15,000 are issued to residents of Pakistan. While these may seem like big numbers, the demand for green cards far exceeds the number available. There are, for example, more than 800,000 Indians working in the United States on temporary work visas waiting for green cards. And more than a million people in Mexico are waiting for family-related green cards, facing an average wait of about twenty years. Unless there are substantial changes in immigration law, most people waiting for permanent-resident status will never achieve it.

So rather than wait for permission that may never come, millions of people decide to take their chances as undocumented immigrants. "A lot of people living in the United States without status, they don't have any options," says Isabel Cueva, an immigration lawyer who crossed the border illegally from Mexico as a little girl. She was fortunate enough to earn permanent resident status through her father, who had been granted amnesty through a temporary program in the 1980s that gave legal status to more than 3 million undocumented immigrants. "People will say, 'Well, just get in line. Just apply, just submit the paperwork. Why don't you just do it the right way?' But there is no way. There's no possibility for a lot of these people here."[7]

Living as an Undocumented Immigrant

Most undocumented immigrants tend to gravitate toward communities with already established immigrant communities. About half of the US immigrant population—both documented and undocumented—lives in California, Texas, Florida, and New York. The rest are scattered across the country, particularly in the Southwest and Pacific Northwest. But states such as Massachusetts, Maryland, Louisiana, and North Carolina have seen significant increases in recent years.

The majority of undocumented immigrants also live in about twenty major metropolitan areas, such as Los Angeles, Houston, and New York City. But as a whole, undocumented immigrants live in cities and towns in all fifty states and the District of Columbia. Even Hawaii has an estimated thirty-six thousand undocumented immigrants, most of whom come from the Philippines and other Asian countries.

Even though an estimated 8 million undocumented immigrants work full-time (about 5 percent of the nation's workforce), finding a job can be challenging for a number of reasons. The language barrier is one problem, but there are other obstacles. Most employers need an employee's Social Security number, for example, which prompts some undocumented immigrants to steal one from someone else or make one up. Many undocumented immigrants are paid in cash, but millions of others apply for and receive a tax identification number (TIN), which allows the federal government to tax their income. A TIN is similar to a Social Se-

Undocumented Immigrants in "White Collar" Jobs

The image of undocumented immigrants is often that of low-paid laborers working on farms, in factories, or in service jobs at hotels or restaurants. Yet according to the Pew Research Center, an estimated one in eight undocumented immigrants has a white-collar job in fields such as sales, management, and even journalism. That figure used to be one in ten as recently as 2007. The shift reflects changes in the national economy, as the number of manufacturing jobs, for example, has declined. But it also reflects the rise of recipients of the Deferred Action for Childhood Arrivals program entering the white-collar workforce and a greater willingness by other undocumented immigrants to pursue opportunities that would have seemed unimaginable a generation ago. Jose Antonio Vargas, a Pulitzer Prize–winning reporter and author, was born in the Philippines but spent almost his entire life in the United States as an undocumented immigrant. He made his status publicly known in a *New York Times Magazine* article in 2011 and has since focused much of his work on reporting on the plight of people very much like himself. "I am an American," he says. "I am just waiting for my own country to recognize it."

Quoted in Matthew Renda, "Undocumented Journalist Describes Immigrant Experience, American Dream," UC Santa Cruz Newscenter, December 11, 2017. https://news.ucsc.edu.

curity number and is equally important to many undocumented immigrants. In some states, it allows an undocumented person to get a driver's license and open an interest-bearing checking account at a bank. TINs also help people establish residency and a paper trail to demonstrate that they have been working, contributing members of society.

Alike yet Different

In some very basic ways, the lives of undocumented immigrants are quite similar to those of people born and raised in the United States. Undocumented kids go to school, play sports, sing in choirs, and hang out with their friends, just like most kids anywhere and from any background. Out in the community, undocumented immigrants shop, attend religious services, go to work, enjoy the beach or parks, watch movies, attend concerts, and otherwise live their lives like their native-born neighbors.

And yet there are countless ways in which the lives of undocumented immigrants diverge from their American-born peers. In many states, for example, unauthorized immigrants cannot get driver's licenses. Jobs that require background checks, such as police officers or government employees, are off-limits. Banking and conducting other financial matters, such as applying for college loans, can also be complicated or risky because providing true information could alert authorities. Undocumented immigrants are not eligible for Social Security, Medicare or Medicaid, and unemployment or disability benefits, and they cannot vote. Leaving the United States, even to visit a relative, could mean never getting to return.

Immigration Reform

The phrases *immigration reform* and *broken system* are used often by policy makers, activists, and voters who recognize the problems with the current state of legal and illegal immigration. There are years-long backlogs of people seeking visas to work in the United States legally. Millions of adults and children cross the border or overstay visas, defying the nation's immigrations laws, often out of fear of living in their dangerous communities back home. Families are separated by immigration officers at the border. Immigration courts are backed up, causing individuals and families to wait in detention centers or spend months on parole awaiting their fates.

And there are countless opinions about how to fix this broken system. Some people want more immigrants to join the American workforce, but others want fewer or none at all. There are calls for pathways to citizenship for undocumented immigrants already in the country, and there are just as many rejections of such an idea. "Our immigration system is a mess,"[8] says Wendy Cárdenas, the daugh-

"Our immigration system is a mess."[8]

—Wendy Cárdenas, a Deferred Action for Childhood Arrivals recipient and immigration activist

18

An ICE official provides assistance as a long line of people wait for their turn in immigration court in 2019 in Atlanta, Georgia. The Trump administration's immigration crackdown has swamped the nation's immigration courts.

ter of undocumented immigrants who has protection under the 2012 Deferred Action for Childhood Arrivals (DACA) policy, which protects many young undocumented immigrants from deportation.

But just what immigration reform looks like is not a clear picture. Public polls show that a majority of Americans want tough border security as well as greater opportunities for immigrants to become citizens. There are also plenty of people who want one, but not the other. Current approaches to toughen border security and aggressively deport undocumented immigrants are not wholly effective and have plenty of opponents. Other options to help undocumented immigrants become citizens are equally controversial. A May 2019 headline in the politics and financial magazine *Fortune* may have summed up a complicated challenge in the simplest but most accurate way: "US Immigration Policy Is Broken, but No One Can Agree on How to Fix It."[9]

CHAPTER TWO

Border Security

In the tiny South Texas town of Falfurrias (population 4,981) the Border Patrol operates a checkpoint in which vehicles are routinely inspected for drugs, weapons, or unauthorized immigrants making their way across the nearby border with Mexico. On a cool Friday night in January 2020, Border Patrol agents examined the back of a semitrailer to find eleven undocumented immigrants hiding between heavy wooden pallets of flour. Another twenty-six unauthorized people were found on other trucks that same night in Falfurrias. All thirty-seven people were taken into custody.

> "The system is well beyond capacity, and remains at the breaking point. This is clearly both a border security and a humanitarian crisis."[10]
>
> —Kevin McAleenan, the CBP commissioner

This scene, and others like it, play out day after day along the nearly 2,000-mile-long (3,219 km) border between the US and Mexico. Between October 2018 and September 2019, 851,508 migrants were apprehended at or near the border—either turning themselves in to claim asylum or hoping to elude the authorities in between ports of entry. That figure is up significantly from recent years, in large part because so many more individuals and families are choosing to claim asylum. In February 2019 alone, more than 76,000 migrants crossed the border without authorization. Many of them were sent to detention centers, which were already approaching their maximum capacity. Shortages of beds, blankets, diapers, hygiene products, and other supplies made conditions even worse. "The system is well beyond capacity, and remains at the breaking point," said Kevin McAleenan, the then CBP commissioner. "This is clearly both a border security and a humanitarian crisis."[10]

The United States has 328 ports of entry, which include CBP stations along the borders with Mexico and Canada as well as various seaports and airports around the country. Official ports of entry are designated and staffed by CBP employees. Ports of entry are where tourists with passports and immigrants with visas have their documentation reviewed before they are allowed to leave the facilities. Ports of entry are also where migrants go when they seek asylum, a type of protection a nation can grant individuals fleeing political persecution or other types of violence in their home countries. An asylum seeker who can prove that he or she would be in serious danger if sent home may be granted temporary

At a Border Patrol checkpoint in Falfurrias, Texas, an agent asks a driver where she is going and whether she is a US citizen. Scenes like this occur at checkpoints all around the country.

permission to remain in the United States, but that decision is made in immigration court.

Although it is relatively easy to track the number of asylum seekers placed in detention or released for an immigration court date later on, it is much more difficult to estimate how many migrants successfully make it across the border in between ports of

VIEWPOINT

Border Security Will Reduce Illegal Immigration

In seeking $18 billion for CBP in 2020, the White House explained in a budget fact sheet that the administration is committed to increasing the enforcement funds to combat illegal border crossings:

Illegal immigration and other illicit materials, particularly illegal drugs, coming across our borders have strained Federal resources and overwhelmed agencies charged with border security and immigration enforcement. High levels of illegal immigration have also impacted the local communities where many of these aliens have settled. The Federal government must employ all lawful means to enforce the immigration laws of the United States and reduce the flow of illegal aliens and illegal drugs into the country. . . .

Overall 2021 funding for CBP ($15.6 billion) and ICE ($9.9 billion) is 11 percent higher than the FY 2020 level.

The Budget proposes sizable investments in a border wall; border security technology and equipment; funding to hire additional CBP and ICE law enforcement officers and support personnel; and increased capacity to detain and deport illegal aliens.

Office of Management and Budget, "Strengthening Border Security: An American Budget," White House 2019 Budget Fact Sheet. www.whitehouse.gov.

entry. The number of border crossings varies considerably, due to factors such as increased border security measures in the United States and Mexico, organized caravans of migrants arriving at the border, and the weather (more crossings or attempts occur in the warmer months than in the winter). In recent years, CBP reports apprehensions between ports of entry ranging from

VIEWPOINT

Border Security Will Not Significantly Reduce Illegal Immigration

Edward Alden, a senior fellow with the Council on Foreign Relations, writes in the *Journal on Migration and Human Security* that focusing on border security is an increasingly less effective tool because visa overstayers and asylum seekers make up the bulk of undocumented immigrants:

> The evidence suggests that deterrence through enforcement, despite its successes to date in reducing illegal entry across the border, is producing diminishing returns. There are three primary reasons. First, arrivals at the border are increasingly made up of asylum seekers from Central America rather than traditional economic migrants from Mexico; this is a population that is both harder to deter because of the dangers they face at home, and in many cases not appropriate to deter because the United States has legal obligations to consider serious requests for asylum. Second, the majority of additions to the US unauthorized population is now arriving on legal visas and then overstaying; enforcement at the southern border does nothing to respond to this challenge. And finally, among Mexican migrants, a growing percentage of the repeat border crossers are parents with children left behind in the United States, a population that is far harder to deter than young economic migrants.

Edward Alden, "Is Border Enforcement Effective? What We Know and What It Means," *Journal on Migration and Human Security*, vol. 5, no. 2, 2017.

about forty-five thousand to more than one hundred thousand people per month. Federal officials estimate that they apprehend around 80 percent of the people trying to cross the border, meaning anywhere from nine thousand to twenty thousand adults and children elude authorities each month, though once they are across the border, arrest and deportation are always possible.

Border Security Effectiveness

With thousands of people going over, under, or through fences; hiding in trucks; landing on US coastlines; or otherwise crossing the border unlawfully, it is clear the current system of border security is not entirely effective. Indeed, it may be impossible to completely seal a border that stretches thousands of miles through largely unpopulated country. But tightening security at the border has long been a high priority for many politicians and law enforcement officials. The federal government spends about $14 billion annually on CBP, including money for walls and fencing, security technology, maintaining a force of CBP officers, and other resources. The CBP budget increases regularly, even as the number of officers has shrunk slightly in the past decade. In 2010, for example, the budget was about $10 billion.

Advocates for tighter border security argue that increased spending on security measures is responsible for the number of unlawful border crossings dropping drastically in recent years from the roughly 1.8 million crossings that occurred in 2000. But a study published in the August 2018 *Journal on Migration and Human Security* suggests that spending billions of dollars more on increased border security, including hard barriers and more surveillance technology, may not be the best approach to reducing undocumented immigration. The researchers instead believe that improved immigration enforcement, such as the detention and processing of asylum seekers and tougher penalties for illegal crossings, is largely responsible for the drop.

But the number of border crossings is still significant enough that conversations about how best to secure the border continue in

Congress and elsewhere. More hard barriers, like walls and fences, are popular with many leaders and CBP officers, but other people support greater investment in technology. "It all comes down to resources," says Border Patrol agent Michael Scappechio. "If the resources are available, it'll help us do our job better. If they're not available, we have to utilize terrain, such as Otay Mountain [in San Diego County, California], as a deterrent, and we have to shift our resources, like our surveillance, like our manpower. If we can put a border barrier [in place], we can utilize our manpower elsewhere."[11]

The Washington Office on Latin America (WOLA), a human rights advocacy organization, recommends, among other solutions, greater investment in sensors and communication equipment, such as integrated fixed towers, remote video surveillance systems, and tethered aerostats, which are inflatable blimp-like craft that contain sensing equipment. WOLA also supports the renovation and expansion of ports of entry and improved staffing to better handle the numbers of unauthorized border crossers and asylum seekers.

Congressman Henry Cuellar, a Democrat from Texas, echoes WOLA's priorities and adds that bolstering US relations with Mexico and encouraging that country to help with the crush of migrants at the border will help. "We will never realize a secure border with Mexico without investing in our border security technology and personnel, and extending border security outward so American borders are the last line of defense, not the first,"[12] he says.

Working the Border

Along the miles of desolate or thinly populated areas of the border, Border Patrol officers use various means to make their rounds. They gallop on horseback in pursuit of fleeing migrants or take to all-terrain vehicles to navigate the rugged landscape stretching from Texas to California. Their airborne counterparts use helicopters and airplanes. Border Patrol agents respond to electronic sensor alarms; operate high-tech surveillance equipment, such as infrared scopes at night; make traffic stops; and escort asylum

A Border Patrol agent searches by helicopter for migrants who have illegally crossed into Texas from Mexico. Agents use high-tech sensors, drones, and other equipment to monitor movements along the border.

seekers and other migrants to centers where they can be cared for medically and detained until the next phase of their immigration process.

When officers encounter someone crossing the border illegally, the situation may involve a lengthy chase, a rescue from a river or other dangerous place, or a quiet encounter involving a frightened and sobbing parent or child. "From being a law enforcement officer to being a rescuer to being a comforter to being a babysitter—I mean, there are so many things that we do," says Border Patrol agent Ramiro Cordero, who is based in New Mexico. "Every time a person enters the United States illegally, a crime has been committed."[13]

In addition to trying to stop migrants from entering the United States, border security measures are also focused on stopping the flow of drugs, weapons, hazardous materials, and terrorists into the United States. The Border Patrol is responsible for patrolling the nearly 6,000 miles (9,656 km) of border along Mexico and Canada as well as 2,000 miles (3,219 km) of coastal waters around the Florida peninsula and the island of Puerto Rico. The US Coast Guard also patrols coastal and inland waterways around the country totaling nearly 100,000 miles (160,934 km). Though much of the Coast Guard's responsibility is related to rescue and safe vessel operation, the agency is part of the Department of Homeland Security (DHS), making the protection of US borders an equally important task.

One of the great challenges in maintaining border security is the hiring and retention of Border Patrol officers. In 2019, the CBP had just over 19,500 agents. In 2017, President Trump called for another 5,000 agents, but within the first year, only 118 new agents had been hired, and only 3 of them were stationed along the southern border. With such a trickle of new hires and a 2019 surge of migrants at the border, President Trump dispatched members of the National Guard and active-duty military troops to the border to assist in security.

Retirements and border agents leaving the agency to pursue other jobs are also cutting into the number of CBP agents on the border. The difficulty in hiring and retaining agents is largely a result of low pay and highly challenging working conditions. They are often stationed in some of the most remote areas of the country—places like Lukeville, Arizona, which has, in addition to a CBP outpost, one gas station, one general store, and a population of about fifty people. "Substandard housing, substandard medical, substandard schools, probably not a job [acceptable to] your spouse or significant other," says Chris Harris, a retired agent and former union representative. "That's a hard sell."[14]

"From being a law enforcement officer to being a rescuer to being a comforter to being a babysitter—I mean, there are so many things that we do."[13]

—Ramiro Cordero, a Border Patrol agent

The stress of regularly dealing with life-and-death situations may also explain the high rate of suicide among CBP agents. Efforts to raise CBP pay to that of other law enforcement agencies have not been successful in Congress, and complaints about insufficient equipment and support is ongoing, says Democratic congressman Joaquin Castro of Texas. "The agents were telling us that oftentimes they're patrolling areas without radio communication or even cellphone communication," Castro says. "It was clear that the agency is not staffed with the medical supplies and training and personnel they need to take care of somebody if they encounter an emergency. . . . So yeah, it is a tough job in that way."[15]

Drones on Patrol

With shortages of personnel, CBP has turned to unmanned aircraft to scan the vast stretches of the US–Mexico border in search of migrants or drugs making their way into the country. CBP operates about a dozen Predator B drones that cost about $17 million each and more than $12,000 per flight hour to operate. CBP is also experimenting with smaller, less expensive drones, but the effectiveness of surveillance drones to help apprehend migrants is questionable.

And because drones can also view US residents and properties along the border, they represent a potential invasion of privacy and a possible threat to the Fourth Amendment rights of US citizens, particularly protection against unreasonable search and seizure. The smaller drones in use also possess facial recognition technology, which could lead to further privacy and mistaken-identity problems. The Cato Institute, a libertarian think tank, noted in a 2018 report on drones at the border, "If CBP's small drones begin to use facial recognition technology, law enforcement agencies run the increased risk of detaining law-abiding people as suspected border crossers."[16]

Although drones, radar, sensors, and other high-tech tools are used up and down the border, it is the construction of a high, fortified wall along much of the southern border that has captured most of the attention when it comes to border security conversations, particularly since President Trump made it a key piece of his campaign pledges during the 2016 campaign for the White House.

Is a Wall Realistic?

President Trump's promised wall to block illegal immigration became a controversial topic, but it proved a popular idea among his supporters. Campaign rallies often included chants of "Build the wall!" as Trump repeatedly promised that Mexico would pay for it. Mexican officials balked at such an idea, and Trump's sought-after wall drew a lot of ridicule, in large part because about 1,300 miles (2,092 km) of the 1,954 miles (3,145 km) of southern border follow the course of the Rio Grande, a formidable barrier itself. Much of the remaining 700 miles (1,127 km) or so of borderland already had a hodgepodge of walls and fences, though Trump promised to replace and expand them all with barriers that would keep out migrants.

President Donald Trump has called for construction of a border wall to block illegal immigration from Mexico. The border already has a mix of fences and other barriers, including this section in New Mexico.

In his first three years in office, only about 83 miles (134 km) of fencing was constructed, and it simply replaced old fencing. Getting the billions of dollars in funding needed for new walls proved a difficult challenge for the president, even among members of his own party, who raised a number of important questions. Would it really be able to keep out determined migrants? How would private property owners respond to plans of putting a giant wall through their ranches, farms, and communities? Environmentalists also noted that impassable walls would affect the migration and natural movement of many species, including the endangered Mexican gray wolf. In a report published in 2018 in the journal *BioScience*, wildlife researchers wrote, "We urge the US government to recognize and give high priority to conserving the ecological, economic, political, and cultural value of the US–Mexico borderlands. National security can and must be pursued with an approach that preserves our natural heritage."[17]

> "There's definitely a conversation to be had about what is actually needed to secure the border. Unfortunately, we're having a conversation just about a wall."[18]
>
> —Theresa Brown, the director of immigration and cross-border policy at the Bipartisan Policy Center

The mission to secure and patrol the southern border goes on 365 days a year, as do the questions about staffing, technology, and whether a giant wall through the deserts and mountains is the best solution to reducing undocumented immigration. "There's definitely a conversation to be had about what is actually needed to secure the border," says Theresa Brown of the Bipartisan Policy Center. "Unfortunately, we're having a conversation just about a wall."[18]

CHAPTER THREE

Should the Dreamers Be Allowed to Stay?

Sharjeel Syed arrived with his parents in the United States before his first birthday. He does not remember his native Pakistan, but he does recall a conversation his father had with him just before he started high school. It was the moment Syed finally learned he and his family were undocumented immigrants. It was the main reason his father had not been able to get a better job, and it would be the cause of the many challenges that lay ahead for Syed. "He told me essentially that I wouldn't be able to go to college unless I was able to get a full scholarship," recalls Syed, who went on to earn a degree from Dartmouth before enrolling in Stanford University's medical school. "I was already motivated, but that just gave me more reason to study."[19] The future physician is hopeful he can also be a US citizen one day. With the protection afforded him under the DACA program, Syed also hoped he would not face the same fear of deportation and live in the shadows the way so many other undocumented immigrants do every day.

President Barack Obama launched DACA in 2012 to protect young people brought to the United States as children from being deported to a country where they have few if any memories and few if any close family members. There are approximately eight hundred thousand DACA recipients, or Dreamers, as they were called when Obama pushed unsuccessfully for the Development, Relief, and Education for Alien Minors (DREAM) Act, which would have granted permanent legal status to young undocumented immigrants. They are students, soldiers, teachers,

President Barack Obama and other officials meet with DACA recipients at the White House in 2013. Obama created DACA to protect young people illegally brought to the United States as children.

doctors, nurses, artists, and professionals in countless fields across the country. Though their DACA status gives them a sense of protection as long as they meet clear-cut eligibility rules, they still live with a permanent sense of uncertainty. They have a limbo-like existence, somewhere between being authorized and unauthorized. "It's really hard honestly," says Edison Suausnavas a DACA recipient and biologist at the University of Utah. "It's an anxiety I live with every day."[20]

For Syed, Suausnavas, and other DACA recipients, life in the United States—the only country many of them have ever really known—exists in two-year increments. Every two years DACA recipients must renew their status under the program. DACA recipients and their allies continue to hope and work to get federal legislation passed that would provide permanent protection for thousands of Dreamers across the nation.

The History of DACA

Because so many children were being brought to the United States by their parents without any say in the matter, immigration advocates sought for years to have some protections for them as they grew up. Attempts to pass federal legislation to protect these young people, such as the DREAM Act, failed to materialize in Congress, despite President Obama's urging.

Rather than be defeated by Republican opposition in Congress, Obama finally issued an executive order on June 15, 2012, establishing DACA and providing at least temporary protection for this generation of undocumented immigrants. An executive order can establish a policy, but it does not have the weight or permanence of a law passed by Congress. A future president can rescind an executive order, as President Trump did with DACA.

But in issuing the DACA executive order, Obama tried to make his case to the nation. He asked Americans to imagine the life the Dreamers lived year after year. In announcing DACA, Obama said,

> These are young people who study in our schools, they play in our neighborhoods, they're friends with our kids, they pledge allegiance to our flag. They are Americans in their heart, in their minds, in every single way but one: on paper. They were brought to this country by their parents— sometimes even as infants—and often have no idea that they're undocumented until they apply for a job or a driver's license, or a college scholarship. Put yourself in their shoes. Imagine you've done everything right your entire life—studied hard, worked hard, maybe even graduated at the top of your class—only to suddenly face the threat of deportation to a country that you know nothing about, with a language that you may not even speak.[21]

To apply for DACA status, a person had to arrive in the United States before turning sixteen and had to be under the age of thirty-one on June 15, 2012. Continuous residency in the United States since June 15, 2007, was also a requirement. DACA recipients also were required to be in school or to have graduated (or received a certificate of completion from high school), or they must have been on active duty or honorably discharged from the armed forces, which includes the Air Force, Army, Coast Guard, Marine Corps, Navy, and Space Force. Having no felony convictions was also necessary.

To renew DACA status, an individual must submit a lengthy renewal form every two years and provide documentation regarding education, employment, residency, and other factors that might affect the person's eligibility. There is also a $495 renewal fee. As long as a current DACA recipient meets the deadline for renewal, has all the necessary paperwork filled out correctly and completely, and can pay the fee, renewal is almost automatic.

Challenging DACA

Just how long DACA will continue to protect the Dreamers is more uncertain than ever, however. In 2017, the Trump administration announced it would end DACA, arguing that Obama's executive order creating the program was unconstitutional. The debate over DACA differs from many other immigration-related issues, primarily because it involves young people who arrived in the United States in the arms of their parents or other family members, as opposed to adults who take the risk of crossing the border of their own free will. Thus, there is some sympathy for the current Dreamers, even from some immigration hard-liners, though they hold little interest in continuing a policy of protecting children who arrive in the United States without authorization. As Elaine Duke, the former acting secretary of the DHS, wrote in a 2017 memo in response to Trump's decision,

> I am very aware of the consequences of this action, and I sympathize with the DACA recipients whose futures may now be less certain. But I am also frustrated on their be-

half. DACA was never more than parole—a bureaucratic delay—that never promised the rights of citizenship or legal status in this country. And for that reason, DACA was fundamentally a lie that left recipients in two-year cycles of uncertainty.[22]

The attorney general in 2017, Jeff Sessions, argued that ending DACA and getting tougher with undocumented immigrants was important because they represented a threat to public safety. "There is nothing compassionate about the failure to enforce immigration laws," Sessions said. "Enforcing the law saves lives, protects communities and taxpayers, and prevents human suffering. Failure to enforce the laws in the past has put our nation

President Trump is pictured in 2017, the same year he announced his intention to end DACA. He contends that the executive order creating the program was unconstitutional.

at risk of crime, violence and even terrorism."[23] Anti-immigration advocates have often tried to link undocumented immigration to high crime. However, a report by the Marshall Project, a nonprofit journalism organization that focuses on criminal justice, shows that areas that have seen a noticeable increase in the undocumented immigration population have actually experienced reduced crime. And a report by the Cato Institute found that in Texas, unauthorized immigrants committed crimes at a lower rate than native-born Americans.

A young protester joins hundreds of others rallying outside the US Supreme Court building as the justices consider the cases for and against DACA on November 12, 2019.

A federal judge blocked Trump's termination of DACA in January 2018, but the government appealed. The US Supreme Court heard oral arguments on three consolidated cases in November 2019. Crowds of DACA recipients and advocates gathered outside chanting, "This is what democracy looks like!"; meanwhile, others took turns watching the hearings in the small public viewing gallery inside the Supreme Court building. At one point, Justice Sonia Sotomayor said the proposed change in DACA legislation "is not about the law, this is about our choice to destroy lives."[24]

While the courts sort out a range of legal arguments for and against DACA, Congress can still take action. Democrats, trying to draft legislation that would ensure permanent legal status and protections for Dreamers, often find themselves up against Republicans who take a traditional, hard-line approach to undocumented immigration.

Leaders opposed to granting undocumented immigrants more rights argue that continuing to endorse DACA status for young people year after year sends a message that unauthorized immigration is tolerated and even endorsed at the federal level. In an editorial published in *The Hill*, a political newspaper, Lora Ries, a former acting deputy chief of staff at the DHS and a senior research fellow at the conservative Heritage Foundation, summed up the view of many DACA opponents: "All Dreamers, however, have one thing in common: They are unlawfully present in this country. Offering amnesty to them—or any other group here illegally—would only encourage more illegal immigration."[25]

"All Dreamers, however, have one thing in common: They are unlawfully present in this country."[25]

—Lora Ries, the former acting deputy chief of staff at the DHS

DACA supporters argue that the many triumphs of DACA recipients—those who have gone on to become doctors battling infectious diseases and teachers reaching at-risk kids in big cities—are proof that the incentives to get an education to remain eligible for DACA benefited the country as a whole. "DACA is one

DACA Benefits the Nation

Xavier Becerra is the attorney general of California. He insists that DACA recipients are vital contributors to the strength of the nation:

> Dreamers—immigrants brought to the United States as young children by their parents without documents—have paid fees, passed background checks and applied for work permits so they could step out of the shadows. They've earned a chance to fulfill their potential, contribute to our economy and enrich our communities. . . .
>
> These young people pursue careers that range from serving our country in the military to joining the ranks of police officers to teaching the next generation of leaders in the classroom. . . .
>
> Instead of frightening young people, we should help them succeed. After all, our children are this nation's most precious natural resource. Why would we expel budding innovators and entrepreneurs to another country and let them boost that economy instead of our own? Why would we deprive our military of committed servicemembers who would help keep us safe?

Xavier Becerra, "DACA Is Lawful and Making America Stronger," *Huffington Post*, September 1, 2017. www.huffpost.com.

of the most successful programs the government has ever implemented," says Jeffrey Davidson, an attorney who represented the University of California in one of the cases before the Supreme Court. "It is consistent with the tradition of similar humanitarian programs going back to the [1950s Dwight D.] Eisenhower administration and it has allowed a huge population to participate in the American society in new and important ways. The rescission of DACA would be a senseless humanitarian catastrophe."[26]

DACA Realities

Because it was created with an executive order, DACA does not have the same binding legal authority as a federally issued stu-

DACA Harms the Nation

Dale Wilcox, the executive director of the Immigration Reform Law Institute, says continuing DACA only encourages future lawbreaking:

> When you reward bad behavior, you get more of it. Following Obama's DACA announcement, radio and print ads began appearing south of the border selling the services of cartel-controlled "coyotes" to teenaged would-be illegal aliens. In a matter of months, the thousand or so apprehensions of unaccompanied juveniles we'd previously been seeing every year surged into the tens of thousands. . . .
>
> Now, thanks to DACA, taxpayers spend hundreds of millions annually to reunite the (mostly) uneducated minors with their (mostly) illegal alien parents in the US. That's money that should have gone to support schools, hospitals, and job-training for American youth. . . .
>
> While "protecting" illegal aliens from the consequences of breaking the law may make them feel good and virtuous, if they get their way on DACA the incentives for further law-breaking at our border will only increase. . . . Given the economic and social pressures here and across the border, we need to ensure against amnesty and the moral hazard it creates, now more than ever.

Quoted in Dale Wilcox, "Why Trump Must End DACA," *The Hill*, January 29, 2017. https://thehill.com.

dent visa or work visa. And it provides no pathway to citizenship. To obtain a green card, a DACA recipient can marry a US citizen and apply for a marriage-based green card while remaining in the country. Serving in the military can also provide a shortcut to a green card for DACA recipients. But most DACA recipients who want a green card on their own must return to their native countries and apply at the US consulate just like everyone else. This means, essentially, moving to the back of the line for the long wait to obtain a visa. "What DACA has done is brought us out of the shadows and allowed us to pursue our careers," says Blanca Morales, a Harvard Medical School student and DACA recipient originally from Mexico. "We can't go back into the shadows. We just can't. We have to find a solution that is going to allow us to contribute even more. And allow us to help make this country a better place."[27]

Apart from the politics and economics surrounding the issue, there is a human cost to keeping families in limbo, especially young people who may lose a parent to deportation, be sent to a country they do not remember, or have no chance at success, no matter how hard they work. Felipe Matos is a Dreamer who came to the United States as a little boy with his mother. They fled the slums of Brazil and he later enrolled in Miami Dade College where he studies economics. He also teaches English to first-graders part time in Miami. He says many of his students are in the same situation he was in, but even at a very young age are being discouraged from even thinking about going to college. "My dream is to become a teacher in an inner city high school, so that I can tell students going through the same thing that they can succeed in life, that they are not worthless, but that they are worth a million," he says. "We can't keep denying young people their dreams."[28]

Nonetheless, there are plenty of people who see no reason why the Dreamers should be offered the same opportunities as other young people who happened to be born in the United States. "A bill that perhaps gives dollars to someone who is undocumented really does not sit well with me. It bothers me. Like many families in Connecticut, my family did it the right way,"[29] said Joe Polletta, a Connecticut state representative and the son of immigrant parents, who opposed a bill allowing Dreamers to access state financial aid dollars for college.

DACA's Future

Though DACA has provided some peace of mind and has afforded thousands of young people the opportunity to go to college and pursue exciting careers, the stress will never completely disappear until Congress enacts legislation to allow the Dreamers to wake up without fear of deportation. For example, Wendy Cárdenas, a twenty-eight-year-old community organizer and DACA recipient from Peru, says she may have to return to Peru if DACA protection is rescinded and there is no way forward to get permanent residence status, let alone citizenship. She and her parents left Peru when she was twelve with hopes of a better, safer life in the United States. "It feels like it would be going backward. My parents came here to give me a better future. If I go back, it's not appreciating all the sacrifices they made for us."[30]

CHAPTER FOUR

Detention and Deportation

When she was just sixteen years old, Meydi Guzman Rivas and her father, Fabio, fled the gang violence and poverty of their native Honduras, only to be stopped by US immigration officials near the US–Mexico border. That was 2018. They were released while their immigration cases worked their way through the courts. But after missing a court date, they were arrested again in October 2019 and placed in immigration detention centers in Illinois, where they had been living.

"Moving between jails they would put chains on my wrists and on my midsection and on my ankles," Meydi recalls. "The water was terrible. It was close to five days initially that I didn't even have any water because it was so terrible."[31] For nearly four months, the eighteen-year-old Crystal Lake Central High School student split her time between two women's detention centers, away from her father and frightened about what her future would bring.

On the outside, school staff members, her friends, and others in the community rallied to raise money to cover her immigration bond payment and allow her to be released while her case continues. "Seeing all the bad things that happen in jail, I was maybe losing my faith and hope,"[32] Meydi says, adding that the support from her school and community helped restore her faith. Not long after she was released, her father was also let go. Now they can only wait and hope that their claims of asylum will be granted, allowing them to stay and not be deported to Honduras.

The story of Meydi Guzman Rivas and her father is not uncommon. The arrest and detention of undocumented immigrants happens every day throughout the United States. But given the sheer number of undocumented immigrants—nearly 11 million adults and children—and the limited resources of immigration authorities, courts, and detention centers, it is not possible to arrest and deport everyone who does not have documentation. Nor is that a goal that most people support. A 2019 survey by the Pew Research Center found that 72 percent of Americans support allowing undocumented immigrants to remain in the country if they meet certain criteria, such as having a job and staying out of trouble.

But until there are significant changes in immigration policy, the federal government will continue to arrest, detain, and deport undocumented immigrants. It is an expensive approach—one deportation costs about $11,000—and it can break up families and instill fear in immigrant communities. But detention and deportation also serve to help authorities enforce immigration laws and possibly deter others who may consider entering the country illegally.

Meydi Guzman Rivas (pictured with her sponsor after being released on bond in February 2020) fled Honduras with her father when she was sixteen. The two were arrested, released, and then rearrested.

Civil and Criminal Charges

By law, anyone who is in the country without permission may be arrested and deported. When people enter the country unlawfully, they can face civil or criminal charges. Even though both types of charges can result in deportation, the distinction is important. A civil charge often results in a fine, a brief stay in a detention center, and eventual removal. A criminal charge, however, can lead to longer incarceration in a federal prison (if convicted), separation from family members, and a criminal record that can make it even more difficult to one day return to the United States and find work as an authorized immigrant.

Physically being in the country without permission is a civil violation. It does not matter whether a person stayed after a visa expired or arrived as a tourist or visitor and then simply remained in the United States. Based solely on that civil infraction, a person will not face criminal charges.

On the other hand, a person confronted while illegally crossing the border can be charged criminally. It's the act of entering unlawfully, rather than simply living on US soil, that is considered the more serious offense. Illegal entrance can include crossing the border between official ports of entry, avoiding examination or inspections, or making false statements when entering or attempting to enter the country. A similar set of laws also makes it a crime to unlawfully reenter the country after having been deported or denied entry previously.

In many cases, an undocumented immigrant confronted by ICE or CBP officers will face a civil charge if that individual was not apprehended actually crossing the border or if he or she does not have a record of being deported previously. But as part of President Trump's efforts to crack down on undocumented immigration early in his administration, more undocumented immigrants were charged criminally for crossing the border, regardless of where they were arrested.

In announcing a zero-tolerance policy toward border crossing, the attorney general at the time, Jeff Sessions, announced in

2018, "If you cross this border unlawfully, then we will prosecute you. It's that simple. If you smuggle illegal aliens across our border, then we will prosecute you. If you are smuggling a child, then we will prosecute you and that child may be separated from you as required by law,"[33] he said. Under the tougher policy, the number of federal criminal arrests for immigration offenses jumped from 58,031 in 2017 to 108,667 in 2018—the highest one-year total in more than twenty years.

> "If you cross this border unlawfully, then we will prosecute you. It's that simple."[33]
>
> —Jeff Sessions, US attorney general

Detaining Children

How the DHS would handle children detained for unlawful entry into the United States became a politically and emotionally charged issue for lawmakers, activists, and average citizens alike after Trump's decision to get tougher on immigration. For many years, most of the people who crossed the border illegally were men from Mexico looking for work in the United States. But as conditions in Central America deteriorated, more women and children began making the trek north to the border.

The numbers of unaccompanied minors soared, too. In 2019 alone, more than seventy-six thousand unaccompanied children were apprehended at or near the Mexican border. The changing demographics of undocumented immigrants required authorities to provide more centers to accommodate women and children. This often resulted in separating babies, toddlers, and older children from their parents—in many cases, with no specified time frame or expectation of when or if the family would be reunited.

News photos and videos of children sleeping on the floors of makeshift detention centers surrounded by chain-link fences horrified people around the world. In 2019, the United Nations High Commissioner for Human Rights, Michelle Bachelet, a

Demonstrators rally in July 2019 in Detroit, Michigan, to protest the Trump administration's policy of separating undocumented immigrant children from their parents. The backlash against this policy led to changes.

doctor and the former president of Chile, condemned the way the United States was handling the surge of migrants at the border. "As a pediatrician, but also as a mother and a former head of State, I am deeply shocked that children are forced to sleep on the floor in overcrowded facilities, without access to adequate healthcare or food, and with poor sanitation conditions," Bachelet said, adding that the damage mentally and physically inflicted upon children in those conditions could have long-lasting and tragic effects. "States do have the sovereign prerogative to decide on the conditions of entry and stay of foreign nationals, but clearly, border management measures must comply with the State's human rights obligations and should not be based on narrow policies aimed only at detecting, detaining and expeditiously deporting irregular migrants."[34]

Undocumented immigrant children are sometimes placed with family members in the United States or are reunited with their parents or guardians either to be deported as a family or to be allowed to stay in the United States as part of a court-ordered asylum decision. In some cases, though, children are placed in the foster care system. Due to the backlash against the family separation policies of the DHS, federal officials have made some changes in an effort to keep families together when possible. But it remains a difficult public policy challenge and one that is at the heart of numerous court cases.

"As a pediatrician, but also as a mother and a former head of State, I am deeply shocked that children are forced to sleep on the floor in overcrowded facilities, without access to adequate healthcare or food, and with poor sanitation conditions."[34]

—Michelle Bachelet, the United Nations High Commissioner for Human Rights

How Cases Are Handled

When ICE or CBP officers take an undocumented immigrant into custody, a few different things can happen. That individual may be asked to sign an agreement to leave voluntarily rather than go through a hearing. The one advantage to this approach is that the person will not have a deportation order on his or her record, which would complicate things later if the person reentered the country and was arrested again or wanted to apply for a visa.

In most other cases, an undocumented immigrant will be detained until a hearing before an immigration judge or will be allowed

Local Law Enforcement Should Help Federal Authorities Round Up Undocumented Immigrants

Matthew Albence, the acting director of ICE, says cooperation between police departments and ICE is essential for public safety:

The fact is: People are being hurt and victimized every day because of jurisdictions that refuse to cooperate with ICE. As law enforcement professionals, it is frustrating to see senseless acts of violence and other criminal activity happen in our communities, knowing full well that ICE could've prevented them with just a little cooperation. . . . The fact is that 70 percent of the arrests ICE makes are at local jails and state prisons across the country. But we used to make more. And we used to get more criminals off the street before sanctuary laws and policies prevented us from doing so, leaving us with no choice but to expend significant digital resources to locate and arrest criminal aliens and other immigration violators out in the community, including at their homes and places of employment—a more dangerous undertaking for our officers and a more disruptive action within our communities. And simply put, a less effective method.

Matthew Albence, "Press Briefing by Acting Director of ICE Matthew Albence," White House, September 26, 2019. www.whitehouse.gov.

out of detention after posting bail. Immigration courts hear civil cases. These civil courts are part of the Department of Justice and operate a little differently than a criminal court. One of the most significant differences is that the accused are not provided an attorney by the government. An undocumented immigrant can have legal representation, but it is at his or her own expense. In some cases, attorneys will volunteer their time to help or nonprofit organizations will provide legal assistance. But for numerous immigrants, many of whom do not have a lot of money for attorney's

Local Law Enforcement Should Not Help Federal Authorities Round Up Undocumented Immigrants

VIEWPOINT

Michael Wildes, an immigration attorney and the former mayor of Englewood, New Jersey, says immigrants will be less likely to work with local police if they might get reported to ICE:

> At first blush, the ability of local police to enforce federal immigration law seems like a viable solution to our nation's challenge of illegal immigration. However, piling the additional duty of immigration enforcement upon our already strained local police will do little more than force illegal immigrants and those who associate with them further into society's shadows. The negative effects which will result thereafter are significant.
>
> First, enforcement of immigration laws by local police will discourage and even prevent undocumented immigrants from accessing police services and will prevent police from the benefit of immigrants' cooperation in fighting and investigating crime. . . . Furthermore, adding immigration enforcement to the gambit of local police duties will strain the resources of local police. The main mission of local police is to prevent and solve local crime. Requiring local police to pick up the slack of federal immigration agencies will only divert crimefighting resources without solving the problem of illegal immigration.

Michael Wildes, "Leave Immigration Enforcement to the Feds," ProCon.org, 2008. https://immigration .procon.org.

fees and speak little or no English—the primary language spoken during the hearings—they are on their own.

A judge can grant asylum if he or she believes that the individual would be in serious danger upon return to his or her country of origin. But the vast majority of undocumented immigrants who appear before a judge are eventually ordered home. According to the Department of Justice, an average of just 11 percent of asylum cases end with an individual being formally granted asylum and permission to remain in the United States.

But just getting to a hearing can take a very long time, due to an overwhelming backlog of cases in immigration courts. The average wait time for a case to be heard is more than seven hundred days, close to two years from the time an individual is arrested until he or she gets to see a judge.

If an undocumented immigrant is being charged criminally, his or her case is heard in federal court. This is a much costlier approach, as the government must provide the person a lawyer. A person facing criminal charges is often held in a federal prison until his or her day in court. A migrant who is charged with "illegal reentry" may instead take a plea deal to a less serious charge of "illegal entry." This avoids the time and cost associated with a trial, but it also prohibits an undocumented immigrant from appealing or challenging the sentence.

Expedited Removal

Another means of speeding up deportations is a program known as expedited removal. Starting in 1996, federal immigration authorities have been allowed to fast-track the deportation of undocumented immigrants in certain situations without going through the normal immigration process involving court hearings and a ruling from a judge. The expedited removal policy initially applied only to people arrested within 100 miles (161 km) of the border and who had been in the country a short time. Migrants who claimed asylum could halt the process temporarily until an asylum officer heard their claim.

But in 2019, as part of President Trump's effort to crack down on illegal immigration, ICE was given the authority to apply expedited removal nationwide and to immigrants who had been in the United States for as long as two years. In a 2019 statement to Congress, then DHS secretary Kevin McAleenan said,

> The new designation adds one more tool for DHS—utilizing specific authority from Congress—to confront the ongoing security and humanitarian crisis on the Southwest

border and throughout the country. We are past the breaking point and must take all appropriate action to enforce the law, along the US borders and within the country's interior. This designation makes it clear that if you have no legal right to be here, we will remove you.[35]

Opponents of the policy immediately objected to granting ICE expanded powers to unilaterally deport people. Once the expedited removal process has started, the individual who has been arrested cannot challenge it in court. Advocacy groups, such as the American Civil Liberties Union (ACLU), are challenging the legality of the policy. "Expedited removal provides less

In 2019 ICE detainees prepare to board a flight in Yakima, Washington. This flight is part of the Trump administration's expedited removal program.

protection than traffic court," says Anand Balakrishnan, an attorney with the ACLU's Immigrants' Rights Project. "It allows a single officer, whether it's a Customs and Border Patrol agent or an Immigration and Customs Enforcement officer, to simply order someone deported within a matter of hours."[36]

"Expedited removal provides less protection than traffic court. It allows a single officer, whether it's a Customs and Border Patrol agent or an Immigration and Customs Enforcement officer, to simply order someone deported within a matter of hours."[36]

—Anand Balakrishnan, an attorney with the ACLU's Immigrants' Rights Project

Since the early days of expedited removal, abuses and mistakes have been made. In the first major review of the policy in 2005, the congressionally appointed Commission on International Religious Freedom found that 15 percent of undocumented immigrants who requested asylum were deported before their claims could be heard. The report noted examples of border agents not asking whether immigrants feared for their safety if they were sent home—a requirement of the law—and other cases in which a person requested asylum but the agent submitted a report saying no such request was made. A 2016 follow-up review by the commission concluded that similar problems still plagued the system.

In September 2019, a federal judge issued an injunction, putting a temporary stop to the expanded expedited removal policy, but as with so many issues surrounding immigration, the matter will continue to be argued in courtrooms, Congress, and in the media for some time.

Sweeping Raids

Another highly controversial tactic in going after undocumented immigrants is a workplace raid that rounds up dozens or hundreds of people at one time. Historically, though, when it comes to farms, factories, and other large employers of undocumented immigrants, law enforcement agencies have often looked the other way because those enterprises relied on undocumented immigrants for labor. And as long as those workers stayed out of trouble and no complaints surfaced, mass arrests and deportations were uncommon. But this highly visible, strong-arm approach has been used off and on for decades, typically when the issue surfaced in the news or in political circles. In 2006, for example, about thirteen hundred undocumented workers were detained at Swift & Company meatpacking plants in Minnesota. Most of them were deported.

Through the years, other mass immigration raids have swept up dozens or hundreds of workers in a single day. President Trump said such raids send a message to migrants considering an illegal crossing of the border. After an ICE raid of seven food-processing plants in Mississippi in 2019, President Trump said, "I want people to know that if they come into the United States illegally, they're getting out. They're going to be brought out. And this serves as a very good deterrent."[37] But Americans are fairly divided on this approach. A July 2019 survey found that just 51 percent of Americans support ICE's sweeping raids, and 35 percent oppose them. One reason for this reluctance is that the people rounded up are workingmen and -women, many of whom have children and have no other brushes with the law.

Leaders in Washington, DC, have long insisted that their highest priorities were individuals who were guilty of other crimes, not just immigration offenses. During President Obama's administration, deportations were primarily used as penalties for undocumented immigrants convicted of violent crimes. In his last year in office, for example, 82 percent of all ICE arrests were of immigrants with a criminal record; this means that only 18 percent of those arrested had committed no other crime. Under Trump's administration just two years later, in December 2018, more than one-third of all ICE arrests were of people with no criminal record.

Apprehending undocumented immigrants at the border or in big workplace sweeps are only two of the ways ICE arrests unauthorized individuals. Immigrants are arrested in their homes, on their way to or from work, or even while taking their kids to school. "We're wasting resources deporting a lot of people who are assets to their communities who have families and mortgages and careers and car notes, and we're going after them with the same vigor that we're going after kidnappers and murderers and bank robbers," says Douglas Rivlin, the communications director for America's Voice, an immigrants' rights group. "That's not a smart approach to law enforcement."[38]

CHAPTER FIVE

Pathways to Citizenship

Sofia Campos's first memory of the United States was her first visit to Disneyland in California, a day filled with music, food, fun, and fireworks. She was six years old, had recently arrived from her native Peru, and was an undocumented immigrant. For years, she was blissfully unaware that she was any different than her friends in Los Angeles. It was not until high school, when she applied for college financial aid and asked her mother for her Social Security number, that she learned she and her family were in the country without authorization, with the threat of deportation over their heads.

Still, she enrolled at the University of California, Los Angeles, commuting on a bus for two hours every day because she had no driver's license. At first, she kept quiet about her status, only sharing it with other undocumented immigrant students who formed an organization on campus to provide each other with support and to share immigration-related information. On the same day Campos graduated, President Obama announced the executive order establishing DACA in 2012.

The announcement gave her hope, but what she and so many other undocumented immigrants want is not just protection from deportation but also a pathway to citizenship so they can be fully engaged in the American experience. "I think the fact that the government has not allowed us to fulfill our potential is very detrimental to our country," she says. But like so many undocumented immigrants who have dreams of unlimited opportunity, Campos clings to the idea that the road ahead will not be as difficult as the road she has traveled so far. Upon the formation of DACA, she recalls, "For once, the question wasn't, 'What now?' It was, 'What's next?'"[39]

Citizenship Through Naturalization

Every year, about 750,000 permanent residents complete the naturalization process and become US citizens. Ceremonies recognizing these achievements are held in communities around the country. New citizens wave small American flags and take an oath of allegiance. And perhaps most importantly, they exchange their permanent resident cards for certificates of citizenship. Tears, smiles, and hugs fill the rooms hosting the ceremonies as patriotic songs play. At a small library in Plainfield, New Jersey, Karla Rodriguez, who moved from El Salvador to the United States with her family when she was four, was granted citizenship along with dozens of others in April 2017. "My mother, brother and me all wanted to become citizens," she said excitedly. "My brother did already and now it's my turn. My mother is next. I am very excited. It means everything. This is the land of the free, and I wouldn't want to be anywhere else. I love this country."[40]

A Pennsylvania man takes the oath of allegiance at a naturalization ceremony. About 750,000 permanent residents complete the naturalization process and become US citizens each year.

But becoming a citizen—a process known officially as *naturalization*—is a much more complicated endeavor than going to a courthouse and filling out some papers. The application itself is a lengthy one that includes many personal questions about residency, character, and a demonstrated commitment to the principles in the US Constitution. Once an application and fee (in 2020 the fee was $725) are submitted and approved, an interview with a US Citizenship and Immigration Services official is scheduled. If that goes well, an applicant must still pass a test of US history and civics. Applicants must also be able to speak, read, and write basic English.

The entire application process takes an average of ten months, but can take two years or more, depending on the location of the office processing the application. Some offices, especially those in regions with large immigrant populations, have a longer backlog of applications to review. Problems with an application, such as missing or conflicting information, failing the citizenship test on the first try, or other complications can also drag out the process or put a person's quest for citizenship in jeopardy.

It Starts with a Green Card

An undocumented immigrant, however, cannot even start the naturalization process without first becoming a green card holder. The naturalization process is open only to green card holders who have been legal permanent residents of the United States for at least five years. Noncitizen members of the armed services can sometimes have a shorter residency requirement.

For undocumented immigrants, just becoming a green card holder means clearing some huge hurdles. DACA recipients have a few options that other undocumented immigrants do not. And a person granted asylum may apply for a green card one year later and then wait for approval. If permanent resident status is awarded, it will take another four years before the naturalization process can begin. An immigrant who overstays a visa may have an easier path, as exceptions are sometimes granted to allow overstayers

Undocumented Immigrants Should Receive a Pathway to Citizenship

Jared Bernstein, a senior economist at the Economic Policy Institute, argues that allowing undocumented immigrants to become citizens greatly improves their economic futures:

> While 9.8 percent of those naturalized are poor, the share for non-citizens is a whopping 21.6 percent. In other words, there is a huge difference between the economic status of immigrants who have become citizens and those who have not. The path to citizenship is also a path out of poverty.
>
> We can thus be confident that an important reason for this difference is the benefits conferred by citizenship and the disadvantages associated with lack of citizenship. It is simply much easier to integrate economically, not to mention culturally and socially, if one is a citizen. . . . We must not let ourselves become a nation of permanent illegal immigrants, who toil in the shadows; nor should we become a nation of "guest workers." We are a nation of immigrants who have trodden the path toward citizenship. A central goal of reform should be to clear that path for those who deserve the privileges, economic and otherwise, of being an American citizen.

Jared Bernstein, "Path to Citizenship and Out of Poverty," Economic Policy Institute, June 29, 2006. www.epi.org.

to adjust their status and, essentially, renew their visas, allowing them to stay on track to meet the time requirements for citizenship application. But a person who crossed the border illegally, is not a DACA recipient, and did not seek asylum has little or no chance of getting a green card, let alone citizenship, under current federal law.

An undocumented immigrant can return home in hopes of then applying for a green card. However, undocumented immigrants who have lived in the United States for more than six months are barred from returning for three years. If they have lived in the United States for more than a year, they are barred for ten years. "People are not going to wait in El Salvador, Mexico and

Undocumented Immigrants Should Not Receive a Pathway to Citizenship

Then-Speaker of the House John Boehner argued that undocumented immigrants could be given legal status, but not citizenship, and only if they pay for breaking immigration laws:

> Our national and economic security depend on requiring people who are living and working here illegally to come forward and get right with the law. There will be no special path to citizenship for individuals who broke our nation's immigration laws. . . . Rather, these persons could live legally and without fear in the US, but only if they were willing to admit their culpability, pass rigorous background checks, pay significant fines and back taxes, develop proficiency in English and American civics, and be able to support themselves and their families (without access to public benefits). Criminal aliens, gang members, and sex offenders and those who do not meet the above requirements will not be eligible for this program. Finally, none of this can happen before specific enforcement triggers have been implemented to fulfill our promise to the American people that from here on, our immigration laws will indeed be enforced.

John Boehner, "Standards for Immigration Reform," *National Review*, January 30, 2014. www.national review.com.

Nicaragua when their families are starving," says Karina Ruiz, the president of the Arizona Dream Act Coalition, which offers legal advice to DACA recipients and other immigrants. "They are not going to wait while the gangs are preying on their children. It's just a decision that people are forced to make in order to pursue happiness, an opportunity for a better life."[41]

The Pathway Debate

Whether a realistic path to citizenship will ever unfold before undocumented immigrants depends on changes in federal immigration law. That means overcoming not just the legal and administrative hurdles surrounding immigration but also some powerful political and social pressures that shape the debate over whether undocumented immigrants should have a pathway to citizenship.

"[The DREAM Act] does nothing to address our crisis. Instead, it tells an entire generation of illegal immigrants that breaking our laws is rewarded."[42]

—Mike D. Rogers, a Republican congressman from Alabama

Opponents see a pathway to citizenship for undocumented immigrants as essentially rewarding criminal behavior. When Democrats in Congress tried to revive the DREAM Act in the summer of 2019, several Republicans said granting a pathway to citizenship for millions of undocumented immigrants sends a dangerous message. "This bill does nothing to address our crisis," said Representative Mike D. Rogers, a Republican from Alabama. "Instead, it tells an entire generation of illegal immigrants that breaking our laws is rewarded."[42]

Similarly, opponents of citizenship opportunities for undocumented immigrants argue that such an approach disrespects the sacrifices of immigrants who went through the lengthy and challenging process of becoming a citizen through established means. Even some immigrants who became citizens are reluctant to support citizenship opportunities for undocumented immigrants. Huy Pham, who arrived from Vietnam as a refugee when he was just a toddler, eventually became a citizen. He and his family had to live in a refugee camp overseas before they could enter the United States, having been sponsored by an American family. "If we can do it the legal way, so can they," Pham says. "We don't have to be creating new programs or giving them preferential treatment."[43]

Economic Impacts

Undocumented immigrants are also seen by some as an economic drain, using tax dollars for entitlements and other services related to education, health care, and law enforcement. However, undocumented immigrants are ineligible for the Supplemental Nutrition Assistance Program (also known as food stamps), regular Medicaid, Social Security benefits, unemployment benefits, and many other federal and state programs. They may be eligible for emergency Medicaid in dire situations and the federal Special Supplemental Nutrition Program for Women, Infants, and Children. The biggest impact undocumented immigrants have is in education because public schools are required to serve all children—regardless of status—in their communities.

The limited-immigration group Federation for American Immigration Reform has estimated that the annual cost of undocumented immigration is about $115 billion a year, but the Cato Institute puts the number at anywhere from $3.3 billion to $15.6 billion. There has been little reliable research to determine how much undocumented immigrants cost the country. David Dyssegaard Kallick, the deputy director

Undocumented immigrants are not eligible for many government social welfare programs, including the Supplemental Nutrition Assistance Program, also known as SNAP or food stamps.

of the nonpartisan Fiscal Policy Institute, says it is difficult to truly measure a person's financial impact on the economy—how much is contributed in taxes and spending compared to how many taxpayer-funded resources that person uses. "Fundamentally I think it's the wrong question," Kallick says of the debate over how much undocumented immigrants cost or contribute. "The right question for undocumented immigrants and any group is, 'Are they paying their fair share of taxes and getting their fair share of service?' You're talking about people who work for very low wages and are excluded from nearly all social services. It takes a real act of will to say they're exploiting us."[44]

Immigration opponents also argue that immigrants push native-born Americans out of jobs. But this is a largely inaccurate picture. At various periods in history, surges in immigration coincided with economic prosperity. In the 1920s, for example, about 14 percent of the people in the United States were foreign born because the country was coming off of two decades of massive immigration, and the economy was booming. In the 1990s, as the economy grew and unemployment dipped, the number of immigrants surged. Even as President Trump sought to clamp down on the numbers of documented and undocumented immigrants in the country early in his administration, he also touted record low unemployment.

In addition, approximately 7.6 percent of immigrants are self-employed, compared to 5.6 percent of native-born Americans, and more than 40 percent of Fortune 500 companies were founded by immigrants. Immigrants, both authorized and unauthorized, tend to take jobs that many Americans either do not want or cannot have. Specifically, these jobs are often low-wage occupations in manufacturing, construction, agriculture, or the service industry. And as most economists would acknowledge, more people working means more money circulating through the economy and more demand for goods and services, which then leads to more jobs. "The average American worker is more likely to lose than to gain from immigration restrictions,"[45] says Giovanni Peri, an economist at the University of California, Davis.

Another common misconception is that undocumented immigrants do not pay taxes. Setting aside the billions of dollars they pay in sales taxes, gas taxes, and other consumer taxes, many undocumented workers also pay federal income taxes. The Internal Revenue Service reports that about 4.4 million undocumented immigrants paid more than $23 billion in federal income taxes, which means they are also contributing to Medicare and Social Security—two programs from which they are unlikely to ever benefit.

> "The average American worker is more likely to lose than to gain from immigration restrictions."[45]
>
> —Giovanni Peri, an economist with the University of California, Davis

A Changing American Culture

Many people believe that allowing millions of people from other countries to become full-fledged citizens would negatively change American culture. Countries such as South Korea and Japan have very strict immigration policies in large part to preserve their distinctive cultures and institutions. US culture, though, is a dynamic collection of influences from around the world, and it has been for a long time. But rising numbers of immigrants from Latin America, Asia, and Africa have triggered many conservative commentators and politicians to use words like *invasion* and other hateful speech to characterize new undocumented arrivals. In April 2019, Fox News commentator Tucker Carlson said, "If you're wondering why America is not anything like the country you grew up in, this is why. Will anyone in power do anything to protect America this time, or will our leaders sit passively back as the invasion continues?"[46]

Advocates for undocumented immigrants see a pathway to citizenship as a solution that keeps families together and affords millions of working people and students the chance to fully participate in the country in which they are living. Those who support a mechanism for letting undocumented immigrants become citizens reason that it would free up millions of federal dollars and other resources currently devoted to deportation efforts every year. And since millions of undocumented immigrants are here working and raising families, the humane approach is to let them become citizens and place on them all the rights and responsibilities of citizenship. "They're already here," says Luis Espinoza, the lead organizer of the Mississippi Immigrants Rights Alliance. "They work. They pay taxes. All of those people who worked at those plants raided by ICE had taxes deducted from their paychecks."[47]

Pathway Proposals

Given the many competing arguments for and against a pathway to citizenship, it is hard to envision a time when the nation's 11 million undocumented immigrants might take a citizenship oath. Most serious proposals for such an idea, or even a scaled-down version that gives some unauthorized immigrants a chance at citizenship, start with the expansion of the green card program.

And since there is already a rigorous process in place for green card holders to become citizens, immigration advocates argue that there is no reason undocumented noncitizens should not have the chance to go through the same evaluation and show a commitment to being an American citizen—even if that means lining up behind those who are applying for citizenship through the traditional process. "We all agree that these men and women should have to earn their way to citizenship," President Obama said in 2013. "But for comprehensive immigration reform to work, it must be clear from the outset that there is a pathway to

"We all agree that these men and women should have to earn their way to citizenship. But for comprehensive immigration reform to work, it must be clear from the outset that there is a pathway to citizenship."[48]

—Barack Obama, the forty-fourth president of the United States citizenship. We've got to lay out a path—a process that includes passing a background check, paying taxes, paying a penalty, learning English, and then going to the back of the line, behind all the folks who are trying to come here legally. That's only fair."[48]

But rather than simply place all undocumented immigrants in line with those seeking citizenship the old-fashioned way, one option may be to let the immigrants decide whether they want green cards or citizenship. In a 2019 report, the Cato Institute proposed three possible solutions to help legalize the status of undocumented immigrants. One of those ideas would give undocumented immigrants a choice between expedited green card status with no chance of becoming a citizen or a lengthier citizenship application process. The researchers at Cato noted that following the 1986 amnesty program, only 41 percent of the immigrants granted legal status went on to become naturalized. This suggests that many undocumented immigrants may want to simply work in the United States legally and without threat of deportation, giving up the right to vote and enjoy other privileges of citizenship.

Other proposals include conditional green cards for undocumented immigrants, who would have to pass background checks, pay a fine (for illegally entering the country), and demonstrate a commitment to education and/or employment. Once those requirements are satisfied, the citizenship application process can begin.

Some immigration advocates suggest a pathway based on longevity, giving undocumented immigrants who have been here for years a shorter, easier route to a green card and the naturalization process. An estimated two-thirds of undocumented immigrants have been in the United States for at least ten years, suggesting a real dedication to remaining in and contributing to the nation.

A Nation of Immigrants

The United States is often referred to as a nation of immigrants. That term often conjures up images of ships carrying new arrivals past the Statue of Liberty in New York Harbor or famous immigrants such as Albert Einstein, Google founder Sergey Brin, and Oscar-winning filmmaker Guillermo del Toro. The Ellis Island immigrants and the famous and successful individuals from other countries are celebrated.

But this nation of immigrants also includes millions of people who are here without permission, often working or going to school while hiding secrets and worrying about their future. It is an untenable situation that demands a solution rather than more years of stress, expense, and political wrangling. But is the solution to deport more immigrants and build walls to keep more from arriving, or to provide a pathway to citizenship for those who want it? Or, is the solution found in some combination of

The Statue of Liberty conjures images of ships carrying new arrivals to America's shores. Today's immigrants include many who came or remained without permission. Their presence continues to spark debate.

all three? There is no shortage of ideas and opinions, and no lack of energy on all sides of the debate.

There is also, despite so many challenges, no shortage of dreams. Emiliano, a fifty-seven-year-old bricklayer from Honduras, who chose not to reveal his last name, says he hopes that working and paying taxes for years in the United States will help when there is a change one day in immigration laws and citizenship becomes a reality for him and millions like him. "You have to hope in something,"[49] he says.

Introduction: In and Out of the Shadows

1. Quoted in CNN, "'He's Not a Criminal': Girl Who Begged for Dad's Release After ICE Raids Reunited with Father," November 8, 2019. www.cnn.com.
2. Quoted in Ari Shapiro, "How Immigration Raids in August Have Changed a Small Town in Mississippi," *All Things Considered*, National Public Radio, November 17, 2019. www.npr.org.
3. Quoted in Shapiro, "How Immigration Raids in August Have Changed a Small Town in Mississippi."

Chapter One: Who Are the Undocumented Immigrants?

4. Quoted in Donald Kerwin, "Press Release: The Center for Migration Studies Releases New Estimates Showing Visa Overstays Exceeded Entries Without Inspection for the Seventh Consecutive Year," Center for Migration Studies, January 16, 2019. https://cmsny.org.
5. Quoted in Krishnadev Calamur, "The Real Illegal Immigration Crisis Isn't on the Southern Border," *The Atlantic*, April 19, 2019. www.theatlantic.com.
6. Quoted in Arijeta Lajka, "MS-13 and the Violence Driving Migration from Central America," CBS News, January 19, 2019. www.cbsnews.com.
7. Quoted in Nicole Nixon, "Why 'Waiting in Line' for Legal Immigration Status Can Take Years," KUER-FM (Salt Lake City), April 12, 2018. www.kuer.org.
8. Quoted in Liz Skalka, "Stamford DACA Recipient Sees 'No Path to Citizenship,'" *Stamford Advocate*, September 8, 2017. www.stamfordadvocate.com.
9. Quoted in Soni Sangha, "US Immigration Policy Is Broken, but No One Can Agree on How to Fix It," *Fortune*, May 21, 2019. https://fortune.com.

Chapter Two: Border Security

10. Quoted in Caitlin Dickerson, "Border at 'Breaking Point' as More than 76,000 Unauthorized Migrants Cross in a Month," *New York Times*, March 5, 2019. www.nytimes.com.
11. Quoted in John Burnett, "Border Patrol Professionals Weigh In on What's Needed: Wall or Fence," *Morning Edition*, National Public Radio, January 10, 2019. www.npr.org.
12. Quoted in Henry Cuellar, "The Answer to Border Security Is Technology, Not Wall," CNN, January 11, 2018. www.cnn.com.
13. Quoted in Marissa Armas, "Day in the Life of a Border Patrol Agent: 'It's Different Nowadays,'" KOAT-TV (Albuquerque, NM), February 3, 2020. www.koat.com.
14. Quoted in Ted Hesson, "The Border Patrol's Recruiting Crisis," *Politico*, February 10, 2019. www.politico.com.
15. Quoted in Hesson, "The Border Patrol's Recruiting Crisis."
16. Quoted in David J. Bier and Matthew Feeney, "Drones on the Border: Efficacy and Privacy Implications," Cato Institute, May 1, 2018. www.cato.org.
17. Robert Peters et al., "Nature Divided, Scientists United: US–Mexico Border Wall Threatens Biodiversity and Binational Conservation," *BioScience*, vol. 68, no. 10, October 2018. https://academic.oup.com.
18. Quoted in Krishnadev Calamur, "$5 Billion Could Buy a Lot of Border Security," *The Atlantic*, January 11, 2019. www.theatlantic.com.

Chapter Three: Should the Dreamers Be Allowed to Stay?

19. Quoted in Gabrielle Redford, "DACA Students Risk Everything to Become Doctors," Association of American Medical Colleges, December 17, 2019. www.aamc.org.
20. Quoted in Alexia Fernández Campbell, "I've Felt a Profound Sadness in the Last Two Years: What Life Is Like for DREAMERS Right Now," Vox, October 28, 2019. www.vox.com.
21. Barack Obama, "Remarks by the President on Immigration," Obama White House Archives, June 15, 2012. https://obama whitehouse.archives.gov.

22. Quoted in Tal Kopan, "Trump Ends DACA but Gives Congress Window to Save It," CNN, September 5, 2017. www.cnn.com.
23. Quoted in Kopan, "Trump Ends DACA but Gives Congress Window to Save It."
24. Quoted in Ephrat Livni, "Sotomayor on DACA: "This Is About Our Choice to Destroy Lives," Yahoo Finance!, November 12, 2019. http://finance.yahoo.com.
25. Quoted in Lora Ries, "Consequences, Not Green Cards, for Young, Illegal Immigrants," *The Hill*, March 12, 2020. https://thehill.com.
26. Quoted in Isabela Dias, "If DACA Ends, It Would Be a 'Catastrophe' for Dreamers," *Texas Observer* (Austin), November 1, 2019. www.texasobserver.org.
27. Quoted in Redford, "DACA Students Risk Everything to Become Doctors."
28. Quoted in Cindy Long, "Undocumented Students Walk the 'Trail of Dreams,'" National Education Association, www.nea.org.
29. Quoted in Jacqueline Rabe Thomas, "Financial Aid for 'Dreamers' Becomes a Reality in Connecticut," *Connecticut Mirror* (Hartford)*, April 25, 2018. https://ctmirror.org.
30. Quoted in Skalka, "Stamford DACA Recipient Sees 'No Path to Citizenship.'"

Chapter Four: Detention and Deportation

31. Quoted in Katie Smith, "Honduran Crystal Lake High School Student Facing Deportation Grateful for Community's Support," *Northwest Herald* (Crystal Lake, IL), March 4, 2020. www.nwherald.com.
32. Quoted in Smith, "Honduran Crystal Lake High School Student Facing Deportation Grateful for Community's Support."
33. Quoted in Robert Moore, "Homeland Security Promises to Prosecute 100 Percent of Illegal Immigration Cases," *Texas Monthly*, May 7, 2018. www.texasmonthly.com.
34. Quoted in UN News, "UN Rights Chief 'Appalled' by US Border Detention Conditions, Says Holding Migrant Children May Violate International Law," July 8, 2019. https://news.un.org.

35. Quoted in Jasmine Aguilera, "Some Undocumented Immigrants Are Now Subject to 'Expedited Removal.' Here's What to Know," *Time*, July 23, 2019. https://time.com.
36. Quoted in Aguilera, "Some Undocumented Immigrants Are Now Subject to 'Expedited Removal.'"
37. Quoted in Maegan Vazquez, "Trump Defends ICE Raid Strategy," CNN, August 9, 2019. www.cnn.com.
38. Quoted in Alan Gomez, "ICE Sets Record for Arrests of Undocumented Immigrants with No Criminal Record," *USA Today*, March 21, 2019. www.usatoday.com.

Chapter Five: Pathways to Citizenship

39. Quoted in Julia Love, "Undocumented 'Dreamers' in College Welcome Immigration Shift," *Chronicle of Higher Education*, July 2, 2012. www.chronicle.com.
40. Quoted in Cheryl Makin, "New Citizens Celebrate with Tears, Smiles and Song," My Central Jersey, April 3, 2017. www.mycentraljersey.com.
41. Quoted in Lee Goldberg, "'People Are Not Going to Wait': Why Legal Path to Citizenship Doesn't Work for Many Migrants," *The Arizona Republic* (Phoenix), June 18, 2017. www.azcentral.com.
42. Quoted in Julie Hirschfeld Davis, "House Votes to Give 'Dreamers' a Path to Citizenship," *New York Times*, June 4, 2019. www.nytimes.com.
43. Quoted in Miriam Jordan, "Most Americans Want Legal Status for 'Dreamers.' These People Don't," *New York Times*, January 25, 2018. www.nytimes.com.
44. Quoted in Jane C. Timm, "Fact Check: How Much Does Illegal Immigration Cost America? Not Nearly as Much as Trump Claims," NBC News, December 22, 2018. www.nbcnews.com.
45. Quoted in Matthew Rozsa, "Economists Don't Agree with Donald Trump That Immigrants Are Taking American Jobs," Salon, August 4, 2017. www.salon.com.
46. Quoted in Robert Mackey, "Donald Trump and Fox News Warned of a Migrant 'Invasion' Before El Paso Gunman Struck," *The Intercept*, August 5, 2019. https://theintercept.com

47. Quoted in Nick Judin, "Immigrants, Activists Call for Rights at the State Capitol," *Jackson (MS) Free Press*, February 25, 2020. www.jacksonfreepress.com.

48. Barack Obama, "Taking Action on Immigration," Obama White House Archives, January 29, 2013. https://obama whitehouse.archives.gov.

49. Quoted in Alexia Fernandez Campbell, "Undocumented Immigrants Pay Taxes, Too. Here's How They Do It," Vox, April 17, 2017. www.vox.com.

Center for Immigration Studies—https://cis.org

The Center for Immigration Studies is a conservative think tank that supports restrictive immigration policies. The website includes news, opinion pieces, and research exploring the issue of immigration and federal immigration policy.

Department of Homeland Security (DHS)—www.dhs.gov

The DHS website covers the many responsibilities of the agency, including border security, deportation, the Coast Guard, and other matters affecting undocumented immigrants.

Migration Policy Institute (MPI)—www.migrationpolicy.org

The MPI website has articles, studies, and resources related to DACA, employment-based immigration, and federal immigration reform. The site also includes helpful explanations and graphs to illustrate current immigration laws and policies.

National Immigration Law Center (NILC)—www.nilc.org

The NILC website shares news about changes to immigration law, ways to volunteer on behalf of immigrants' rights, and many resources for documented and undocumented immigrants.

Nolo—www.nolo.com

Nolo provides legal information about a wide range of subjects, including immigration. Articles cover subjects such as immigration court, a person's rights when confronted by an immigration officer, and applying for citizenship.

US Customs and Border Protection (CBP)—www.cbp.gov

The CBP website explains the many duties of the agency, including its role in dealing with undocumented immigrants in the country and those stopped at the border and other ports of entry.

Books

John Allen, *Detaining and Deporting Undocumented Immigrants*. San Diego: ReferencePoint, 2020.

Ilona Bray, *Immigration Made Easy*. Berkeley, CA: Nolo, 2019.

Aviva Chomsky, *How Immigration Became Illegal*. Boston: Beacon, 2017.

Judy Dodge Cummings, *Immigration Nation: The American Identity in the Twenty-First Century*. White River Junction, VT: Nomad, 2019.

Kathleen Krull, *American Immigration, Our History, Our Stories*. New York: HarperCollins, 2020.

Barbara Sheen, *The Dreamers and DACA*. San Diego: ReferencePoint, 2020.

Internet Sources

Claire Felter, Danielle Renwick, and Amelia Cheatham, "The U.S. Immigration Debate," Council on Foreign Relations, February 24, 2020. www.cfr.org.

Elaine Kamarck and Christine Stenglein, "How Many Undocumented Immigrants Are in the United States and Who Are They?," Brookings Institution, November 12, 2019. www.brookings.edu.

Jens Manuel Krogstad, Jeffrey S. Passel, and D'Vera Cohn, "5 Facts About Illegal Immigration in the U.S.," Pew Research Center, June 12, 2019. www.pewresearch.org.

Library of Congress, "Immigration: Primary Source Sets." www.loc.gov.

James Roland has written more than a dozen books for young people about subjects ranging from history and science to careers and social issues. He was a longtime newspaper reporter and editor before becoming an author. He is married with three children.